Starting
ENGLISH
with a
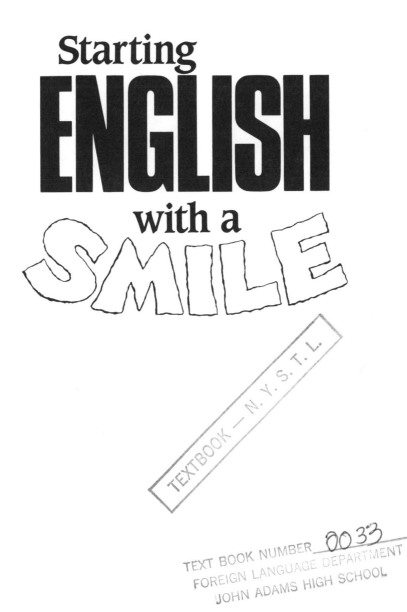

Starting ENGLISH with a SMILE

Light-hearted Stories and
Reading Skills for
Low-beginning and
Beginning Students

Barbara Zaffran
Staff Development Specialist
in ESL and Native Languages,
New York City

National Textbook Company
a division of *NTC Publishing Group* • Lincolnwood, Illinois USA

To Dany for his cooperation,
Sam Leve for his inspiration,
and my mother, Betty L. Hook,
for her unflagging encouragement
and support

1994 Printing

Published by National Textbook Company, a division of NTC Publishing Group.
©1993 by NTC Publishing Group, 4255 West Touhy Avenue,
Lincolnwood (Chicago), Illinois 60646-1975 USA.
Manufactured in the United States of America.
Library of Congress Catalog Card Number: 92-60098

3 4 5 6 7 8 9 0 VP 9 8 7 6 5 4 3 2

Contents

Introduction

To the Student

This is a collection of short stories. Most of the stories talk about students like you. They tell about many interesting people and funny events. Maybe you can see yourself in the stories. Maybe you can think of your own stories to tell or write about.

Read and enjoy the stories in *Starting English with a Smile*. After you finish this book, you might like to read the next two books in this series: *English with a Smile* and *More English with a Smile* as well as many other books. You'll build your English-language skills and have fun as well.

To the Teacher

Many of the stories in this book are based on commonly encountered humorous incidents and experiences. Readers should be able to identify with a variety of characters and situations described in the stories. Some of the stories offer a thematic connection to the school curriculum, for example, students read and talk about world and American history, art, music, language, and culture. Other stories focus on daily life, both inside and outside of the classroom: birthday celebrations, corresponding with family and friends, favorite foods, pen pals, traveling, money, sports, and more.

Each story develops listening, speaking, reading, writing, and critical-thinking skills through a communicative approach. Students are asked to take an active part in each chapter by developing personal vocabulary lists, role playing situations based on the stories, contributing prior knowledge, interacting with characters, and comparing the stories to their feelings and experiences. In addition, practice in content-area skills, such as working with numbers in charts and graphs, collecting data, and so on, has been integrated into each chapter.

There is a structural base to the sequence of stories that can be emphasized at the teacher's discretion. All structures are taken from the stories and are presented in meaningful contexts.

A variety of activities to foster student-student interaction are presented. In addition, learners will become familiar with various questioning formats often used on tests.

In some instances, proverbs, puns, and idioms have been used as titles or as bases of story plots. You may want students to explore the meanings and usages of the phrases and check their own heritage for similar ideas or sayings.

It is hoped that both you and your students enjoy reading the stories and that your students will use them as bases for expanding their knowledge of themselves and the English language.

Story 1

That Takes the Cake

Before You Read

A. Write the correct word or phrase under each picture.

birthday cake   candle   grandma   singing   teenage girl

_____   _____   _____   _____   _____

B. What does the word **birthday** make you think of? Write some words for each category.

activities

_____

_____

feelings

_____

_____

food

_____

_____

people

_____

_____

C. 1. Look at the picture below. Write all the words that you
know.

_____   _____   _____

_____   _____   _____

_____   _____   _____

_____   _____   _____

_____   _____   _____

2. Choose three words. Write a sentence with each word.
Read your sentences to a classmate.

D. Look at the picture. Then try to guess what happens next. Draw a picture and write a sentence about it. Explain your picture to a classmate.

That Takes the Cake

Teenage girl: How old are you, Grandma?

Grandmother: I'm 20 years old. How old are you?

Teenage girl: I'm 16. My birthday is February 28, every year.

Grandmother: My birthday is February 29, every four years. That's how I stay so young.

While You Read

A. 1. Complete the chart.

	Teenage Girl	Grandma	You
age			
month of birth			
day of birth			

    2. Using the information from the chart, write three sentences. Read your sentences to a classmate.

B. Read the story again. Write the words that you do not know. Work with a classmate to find the meanings of the new words. Use a dictionary if you need help.

_____   _____

_____   _____

_____   _____

_____   _____

C. Complete these sentences.

1. How _____ are you?

2. _____ 20 years old.

3. My _____ is February 29.

4. February 29 comes every _____ years.

After You Read

Comprehension Check

A. 1. Sit in groups of five. Answer the questions and complete the chart together.

- How old are you?
- When is your birthday?

Students	Age	Birthday
1		
2		
3		
4		
5		

2. Find the average age of your group.

B. 1. Write the months of the year.

_____ , February, _____ , _____ , _____ ,

_____ , _____ , _____ , _____ ,

_____ , _____ , _____

2. Make a bar graph. Show how many students in your class
have birthdays in each month.

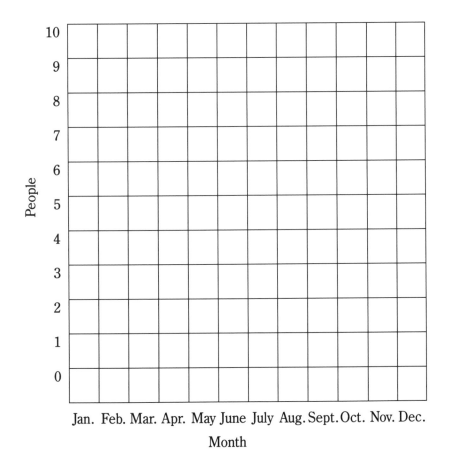

C. Write **T** if the sentence is correct and **F** if the sentence is false. Correct the sentence if it is false.

1. Grandma is twenty years old.
2. The teenage girl's birthday is in March.
3. Grandma's birthday is February 29.
4. February 29 comes every four years.
5. There is/was a February 29 this year.

D. As your teacher reads the story, fill in the missing words.

— How _____ are you, _____?

— I'm _____ years old. _____ old are you?

— I'm _____. My _____ is _____ 28,

every year.

— My _____ is _____ 29, every four years.

That's _____ I stay so _____.

Structure Practice

A. Match each question with the correct answer.

1. How old is she?	a. I am 17.
2. How old am I?	b. Lucy and Ahmed are 20.
3. How old are we?	c. You are 14.
4. How old are they?	d. The dog is 13.
5. How old are you?	e. Joseph is 12.
6. How old is he?	f. Mrs. Lee is 25.
7. How old is it?	g. You and I are 15.

B. Use a contraction to complete each sentence.

I'm   You're   He's   She's   It's   We're   They're

1. I am John. _____ 16 years old.

2. She is Julia. _____ 18 years old.

3. He is Alaatin. _____ 26 years old.

4. They are my friends. _____ 19 years old.

5. We are students. _____ 17 years old.

6. You are young. _____ 11 years old.

7. This is my car. _____ 4 years old.

C. 1. Complete the questions with these words.

happy   how   old   tall

a. How _____ are you?

b. How _____ are you?

c. _____ _____ are you?

2. Ask a classmate each question. Write your classmate's answers.

Story 2

Post It, Please!

Before You Read

A. Write the correct word or phrase under each picture.

letter   mail   mail carrier

_____   _____   _____

B. Complete the sentences.

1. A person who delivers mail is a _____.

2. We write _____ to our families and friends.

3. Letters, cards, and packages are called _____.

C. 1. What does the phrase **mail carrier** make you think of?
   Write some words for each category.

job

_____

_____

mail carrier

clothes

_____

_____

good points

_____

_____

bad points

_____

_____

2. Write three sentences using some of your ideas. Share your sentences with a classmate.

D. Write three or four sentences about what you see in the picture.

Post It, Please!

Boy:	Excuse me, please.
Mail carrier:	May I help you?
Boy:	Yes. When does the mail go to Guatemala from here?
Mail carrier:	The mail goes to Guatemala every day.
Boy:	Everyday? Let's see. Sunday, Monday, Tuesday, Wednesday, Thursday, Friday, Saturday. When is **everyday?**
Mail carrier:	Every day means all of those days. Here, give your letter to me. I'm taking this mail to the post office now.

While You Read

A. Complete the dialogue.

Boy:	_____
Mail carrier:	May I help you?
Boy:	_____
Mail carrier:	The mail goes to Guatemala every day.
Boy:	_____
Mail carrier:	Every day means all of those days. Here, give your letter to me. I'm taking this mail to the post office now.

B. Act out the dialogue with a classmate. Take turns playing the boy and the mail carrier.

C. Write a sentence that tells why the boy is confused. What doesn't he understand?

After You Read

Comprehension Check

A. 1. Circle the words that describe the boy. Then write three sentences about the boy.

a. old/young
b. tall/short
c. friendly/unfriendly

d. nice/not nice
e. confused/confident
f. polite/rude

2. Circle the words that describe the mail carrier. Then write three sentences about the mail carrier.

a. old/young
b. tall/short
c. friendly/unfriendly

d. nice/not nice
e. confused/confident
f. polite/rude

3. Show your sentences to a classmate.

B. 1. Put the days of the week in order and write them on the calendar.

**Friday   Monday   Saturday   Sunday   Thursday
Tuesday   Wednesday**

July

		1	2	3	4	5
6	7	8	9	10	11	12
13	14	15	16	17	18	19
20	21	22	23	24	25	26
27	28	29	30	31		

2. Write the abbreviations for the days of the week.

Sunday   _____

Monday   _____

Tuesday   _____

Wednesday   _____

Thursday   _____

Friday   _____

Saturday   _____

C. Answer the questions.

1. Where is the post office nearest your home?
2. Where is the mailbox nearest your home?
3. Who delivers your mail?
4. Does the mail carrier bring mail to your home every day?
5. Do you write letters? If so, to whom? Where do you mail them?

Structure Practice

A. Replace the underlined words with pronouns.

he   it   she   they   we

1. The boy talks to the mail carrier.
2. The mail carrier helps the boy.
3. The mail goes to Guatemala every day.
4. The boy and I mail letters every day.
5. The boy and the mail carrier talk.

B. Interview a classmate. Circle his or her answers. Report to the class.

1. How often do you come to school?
   a. every day   b. every other   c. once a month
                          week

2. How often do you study?
   a. once a week   b. every night   c. every Saturday
                                              and Sunday

3. How often do you write letters?
   a. every week   b. every month   c. never

4. How often do you talk on the telephone?
   a. every day   b. every week   c. every month

5. How often do you read a book?
   a. every week   b. every month   c. every year

C. 1. Write a question for each answer.

   Example: The mail goes to Guatemala every day.
   Does the mail go to Guatemala every day?

   a. The boy goes for a walk.
   b. The mail carrier goes to the mailbox.
   c. The mail goes to the post office first.

   2. Replace the underlined words with the pronoun **he, she,** or **it.** Then write a question for each answer.

   Example: The mail goes to Guatemala every day.
   It goes to Guatemala every day.
   Does it go to Guatemala every day?

   a. The boy goes for a walk.
   b. The mail carrier goes to the mailbox.
   c. The mail goes to the post office first.

   3. Compare your answers for parts 1 and 2.

Eat, Drink, and Be Merry

Before You Read

A. What does the phrase **to eat** make you think of? Write some words for each category.

what
_____
_____

when
_____
_____

where
_____
_____

why
_____
_____

B. Circle the correct word or phrase for each picture.

1.

    a. spinach salad   b. ice   c. grilled swordfish

2.

    a. peanut butter   b. spaghetti and   c. fish and chips
       and jelly   meatballs

3.

   a. soup   b. salad   c. bread

4.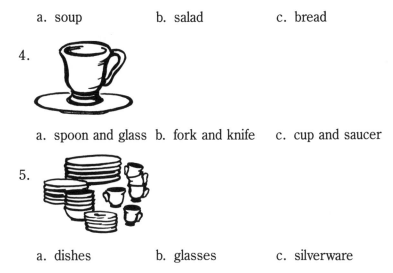

   a. spoon and glass b. fork and knife   c. cup and saucer

5.

   a. dishes   b. glasses   c. silverware

C. Look at the picture on page 16. Then read the sentences and circle the one that is false.

   1. Three boys are eating.
   2. Three boys are wearing glasses.
   3. They are in a restaurant.
   4. One boy is eating soup.

D. The boys are talking about their favorite foods. Try to guess what they are saying.

   1. First boy:
   2. Second boy:
   3. Third boy:

Eat, Drink, and Be Merry

Wen: What are your favorite dishes, Alaatin?

Alaatin: My favorite dishes are spinach salad and spaghetti and
meatballs. What are your favorite dishes, Bori?

Bori: My favorite dishes are lentil soup and grilled swordfish.
What are your favorite dishes, Wen?

Wen: My favorite dishes are a cup and a saucer.

While You Read

A. 1. Complete the chart.

Name	Favorite Foods
Alaatin	
Bori	
Wen	

2. Write three sentences using the information from the chart.

B. Compare your answers in activity D on page 15 with the answers you find in the story. What are the boys really saying?

1. First boy:
2. Second boy:
3. Third boy:

C. Read the story again. Write the words that you do not know. Work with a classmate to find the meanings of the words. Then write sentences with the new words.

_____   _____

_____   _____

_____   _____

_____   _____

After You Read

Comprehension Check

A. Write two questions that you want to ask the boys. Then show your questions to a classmate and ask him or her to answer them.

_____

B. 1. Complete the chart in groups of three.

	Favorite Dish	
	In Native Country	In the United States
You		
Classmate 1		
Classmate 2		

2. Complete the sentences.

a. In our native countries, our favorite dishes were

_____, _____, and _____.

b. In the United States, our favorite dishes are

_____, _____, and _____.

C. Give two meanings for the word **dish.**

D. Bring a recipe for your favorite dish to share with the class.

Structure Practice

A. Choose the best word to complete each sentence.

my   your   his   her   our   their

1. I'm Hiroe. _____ favorite dishes are roast beef and cherry pie.

2. We're Joe and Ahmed. _____ favorite dishes are couscous and bourekas.

3. She's Jessica. _____ favorite dishes are spinach salad and chicken Kiev.

4. They're Suzuki and Yoichi. _____ favorite dishes are miso soup and sushi.

5. He's Ricardo. _____ favorite dishes are vegetable soup and lamb stew.

B. Complete each sentence with **is** or **are.**

There _____ many kinds of food. My favorite food

_____ pizza. Pizza _____ good to eat. It

_____ made of bread, cheese, and tomato sauce.

Sometimes meat or vegetables _____ on the pizza, too.

_____ there any pizza stores near your house?

C. Write five sentences with **is** or **are.**

Pen Pals Meet

Before You Read

A. 1. What is a date? What does the word **date** make you think of? Write some words for each category.

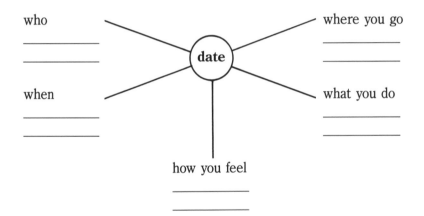

who
_____
_____

where you go
_____
_____

when
_____
_____

what you do
_____
_____

date

how you feel
_____
_____

2. Write four sentences using some of your ideas.

B. Write the correct words under each picture.

happy	strong
old	tall
sad	weak
short	well dressed
sloppy	young

20

1. _____ _____   2. _____ _____

3. _____ _____   4. _____ _____

5. _____ _____

C. 1. Write all the words that you can about the picture on page 23.

_____   _____

_____   _____

_____   _____

_____   _____

_____   _____

2. Write three or four sentences about the picture.

D. Look at the picture. What do you think will happen next? Talk about your ideas with a classmate.

Pen Pals Meet

Sharon: I have a date tonight.

Tanya: With whom?

Sharon: With my pen pal, Alex.

Tanya: What's he like?

Sharon: He's very nice. Look! This is his picture.

While You Read

A. 1. Complete the chart. Use the picture and your imagination.

	Sharon	Alex	You
age			
height			
weight			
color of hair			
color of eyes			
clothing			

2. Write three sentences using the information from the chart.

B. Read the story again. Underline the words that you do not know. Then write them. Work with a classmate to find their meanings. Use a dictionary if you need help.

_____   _____   _____

_____   _____   _____

C. Number the sentences in the correct order.

_____ Sharon receives a letter from a pen pal.

_____ Sharon tells her friend.

_____ Sharon answers the letter.

_____ The boy calls Sharon.

_____ Sharon has a date tonight.

After You Read

Comprehension Check

A. 1. Who is behind the door? Draw a picture of a friend.

2. Explain your picture to a classmate.

B. 1. Make a list of words that describe you.

_____	_____	_____
_____	_____	_____
_____	_____	_____
_____	_____	_____
_____	_____	_____

2. Use some of the words to tell a pen pal about yourself.

C. Answer these questions about Sharon's date. Use your imagination.

1. What's his name?
2. Where is he from?
3. Where do they go?
4. What do they see?
5. What time do they come home?

D. Carlos is asking Roda for a date. Complete the dialogue.

Carlos: Are you busy _____?

Roda: _____

Carlos: Let's go to _____.

Roda: _____

Carlos: What time do you want me to get you?

Roda: _____

Carlos: What time must you be home?

Roda: _____

Carlos: See you _____.

Roda: _____

Structure Practice

A. Match each question with the correct answer.

1. Does Sharon have a boyfriend?
2. Is Sharon happy about her date?
3. Is Tanya going with Sharon?
4. Is Alex Sharon's pen pal?
5. Does Sharon like her pen pal?

a. Yes, she is.
b. Yes, she does.
c. Yes, he is.
d. No, she doesn't.
e. No, she isn't.

B. What does Sharon say to her pen pal? Complete each question with **how, what,** or **where.**

1. Sharon: _____ are you?

   Pen pal: I'm fine, thanks.

2. Sharon: _____'s your sister's name?

    Pen pal: Jenny.

3. Sharon: _____ are you going on Saturday?

    Pen pal: I'm going to the football game.

4. Sharon: _____ do you live now?

    Pen pal: I live at 1302 Newkirk Avenue.

5. Sharon: _____ sports do you like?

    Pen pal: _____

C. Rewrite the paragraph using these adjectives.

pretty	red	green	tall
black	thick	brown	light

Elizabeth is a girl. She has hair and eyes. Tonight she has a date. His name is Kenny. He's a boy. He has hair and eyes.

Story 5

It's Raining, It's Pouring

Before You Read

A. Write the correct word under each picture.

cat   cloud   dog   lightning   puddle
rain boots   raincoat   umbrella

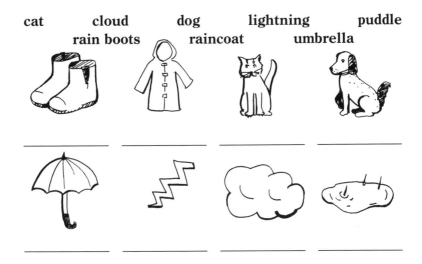

B. 1. What does the word **weather** make you think of? Write some words for each category.

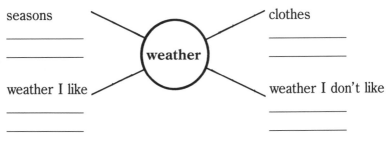

2. Write four or five sentences using some of your ideas.

C. Look at the picture. Write all the words that you know.

————————————————— —————————————————

————————————————— —————————————————

————————————————— —————————————————

————————————————— —————————————————

————————————————— —————————————————

D. Write three questions about the picture. Ask a classmate to answer them.

E. Look at the picture and try to guess what the story is about. Talk about your ideas with a classmate.

It's Raining, It's Pouring

Tomer: Hi, Nadav. How's the weather in New York? It's very hot here in Tel Aviv.

Nadav: It's cool and it's raining cats and dogs. I don't get wet because I wear a raincoat and boots and I carry an umbrella.

Tomer: But you can still get hurt. Cats and dogs are heavy!

Nadav: English is a funny language. **It's raining cats and dogs** doesn't mean anything about cats or dogs. It means that it is raining very, very hard!

While You Read

A. 1. Complete the chart by putting an **X** under the correct name.

	Nadav	Tomer
lives in New York		
makes phone call		
talks about hot weather		
talks about cool weather		
doesn't understand English well		
lives in Israel		

2. Write three or four sentences using the information from the chart.

B. Find the sentence in the story in which:

1. Tomer tells about the weather in Tel Aviv.
2. Nadav says that it's raining very hard.
3. Nadav tells what he wears.
4. Tomer asks about the weather in New York.

C. As you read, complete the sentences.

1. How's the _____ in New York?

2. It's _____ and it's _____ _____ and dogs.

3. I don't get _____ because I wear a _____ and
_____ and I carry an _____.

4. Cats and dogs are _____.

5. English is a _____ language.

After You Read

Comprehension Check

A. 1. Circle the word that doesn't belong in each line.
   a. hot, cold, language, weather
   b. umbrella, cats, dogs, animals
   c. boots, dog, raincoat, umbrella
   d. New York, Tel Aviv, Moscow, English
2. Write a sentence using the remaining three words in each
   line.

   Example: a. The <u>weather</u> can be <u>hot</u> or <u>cold</u>.

B. Answer the questions.

   1. How is the weather in New York?
   2. How is the weather in Tel Aviv?
   3. Do you like hot, sunny weather or cool, rainy weather?
      Why?
   4. In your native language, how do you express the idea **it's
      raining cats and dogs?**

C. 1. In the United States, there are four seasons: spring,
      summer, fall, and winter. What months are in each season?
      Where you live, what is the weather like in each season?

What kinds of clothes do you wear in each season? What do you do in each season? Use your answers to complete the chart.

United States

	Spring	Summer	Fall	Winter
months				
weather				
clothes				
activities				

2. Write four sentences using the information from your chart.

D. 1. What are the seasons like in your native country? Complete the chart.

Native Country

	Spring	Summer	Fall	Winter
months				
weather				
clothes				
activities				

2. Write four sentences using the information from your chart.

E. Show your charts from activities C and D to a classmate. Talk about which things on your charts are the same and which things are different.

Structure Practice

A. Underline all the contractions in the story. Write the contractions and the words that they stand for.
Example: <u>he's</u>   <u>he is</u>

_____   _____

_____   _____

_____   _____

_____   _____

B. Complete each sentence with **a** or **an** if necessary.

1. I have _____ umbrella.

2. He has _____ raincoat.

3. We have _____ boots.

4. English is _____ funny language.

5. She likes _____ icy, cold days.

C. Write a question for each answer.

1. It's hot in Tel Aviv.
2. I have an umbrella.
3. English is a funny language.
4. It rains hard in the spring.
5. We like rainy weather.

Story 6

It's Greek to Me

Before You Read

A. 1. What does the word **Egypt** make you think of? Write some words for each category.

people

land

history

places to visit

2. Write three sentences using some of your ideas.

B. Complete the paragraph by writing the correct word for each picture.

graffiti   Greek   hieroglyphics
museum   pyramid   report

The students are writing a . They are at the

(1)

 . They are looking at a stone from an Egyptian

(2)

 . There is writing on the stone. Guillermo says that

(3)

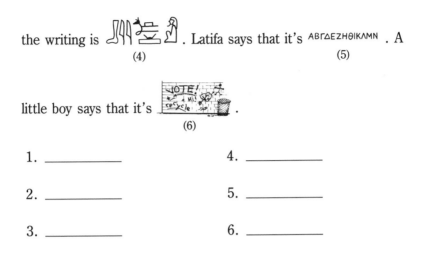

the writing is ____ . Latifa says that it's ΑΒΓΔΕΖΗΘΙΚΛΜΝ . A
     (4)   (5)

little boy says that it's ____ .
                           (6)

1. _____   4. _____

2. _____   5. _____

3. _____   6. _____

C. Look at the picture on page 36 and answer the questions.

    1. Where are the students?
    2. What are they looking at?
    3. What are they trying to read?
    4. What is the little boy doing?

It's Greek to Me

Keisha, Guillermo, and Latifa must write a report about Egypt for their world history class. They are at the museum. They are looking at a stone from an Egyptian pyramid. They are trying to read the writing on the stone.

"Can you read this?" asks Keisha.

"No, can you?" answers Latifa.

"I can't read it either," says Keisha.

"Our teacher says it's hieroglyphics," says Guillermo.

"No, it looks like Greek to me," says Latifa.

"You're both wrong," says Keisha. "It's cuneiform."

"You're all wrong," says a little boy who is standing nearby. "It looks like graffiti to me."

While You Read

A. Find the answers to these questions in the story.

    1. Where are the students?
    2. What country are they studying?
    3. What are the students looking at?
    4. What are four kinds of writing?

B. What do you want to know about Egypt? Write three questions.

C. What two things does the story tell you about the stone? Write two sentences about the stone.

D. 1. Read the story again. Write the words that you do not know. Work with a classmate to find their meanings. Use a dictionary if you need help.

_____   _____

_____   _____

_____   _____

_____   _____

_____   _____

2. Copy the sentences containing the new words.

After You Read

Comprehension Check

A. Sit in groups of three. Ask your classmates the questions you wrote for activity B on page 36. How many of the questions can they answer? Ask your teacher if you need help.

B. 1. Look at the picture on page 36. Try to guess what the hieroglyphics on the stone are about.

2. Make up your own hieroglyphics and write a note to a classmate.

C. 1. Name some different kinds of museums. What can we see in each?

Kind of Museum	Kinds of Exhibits

2. What kind of museum do you want to visit? Why? Talk with a classmate.

Structure Practice

A. 1. Can you do these things? Write a complete answer that starts with **Yes, I can** or **No, I can't.**

Example: ride a bike
Yes, I can ride a bike.

a. read hieroglyphics
b. visit a museum
c. write a report
d. read graffiti
e. live in a pyramid

2. Now ask a classmate questions about the activities listed above. Your classmate must answer with **Yes, I can** or **No, I can't.**

Example: Can you read hieroglyphics?
No, I can't.

B. Answer the questions in complete sentences.

1. What are the students writing?
2. What are they visiting?

3. What are the teenagers trying to read?
4. How many people are looking at the stone?
5. Who is talking to the three students?

C. Fill in the blanks with adjectives to make the story more interesting.

Keisha, Guillermo, and Latifa must write a _____

report about Egypt. They are now at the _____

museum. They're looking at a _____ stone from a

pyramid. There is _____ writing on the stone. The

writing is _____ difficult to read. A _____ boy is

looking at the _____ writing, too.

The Right Degree

Before You Read

A. 1. What does the word **suitcase** make you think of? Write some words.

suitcase

2. Write three sentences using some of your ideas.

B. Look at the picture on page 43 and answer the questions. Use your imagination.

1. How is Dany dressed?
2. How are the other people dressed?
3. Why is Dany dressed this way?
4. Where are the people in this picture?
5. What is this story going to be about?

C. Look at this family tree.

Now complete the sentences by writing the correct relationships. Use words from this list.

grandfather	grandmother
father	mother
uncle	aunt
brother	sisters
son	daughters
nephew	niece
cousins	child

1. Dany is Alan and Barbara's _____.

2. Regine is Dany's _____.

3. Claude is Dany's _____.

4. Nathy, Judith, Galith, and Myriam are Dany's _____.

5. Nathy is the girls' _____.

6. The girls are Nathy's _____.

7. The girls are Claude and Regine's _____.

8. Nathy is their _____.

9. Alan is Dany's _____.

10. Barbara is Dany's _____.

11. George and Jeanne are the children's _____ and _____.

12. Dany is Claude and Regine's _____.

13. Judith is Alan and Barbara's _____.

The Right Degree

1   The phone rings. It's Dany's aunt. She invites him to visit for a week. Dany is happy. He wants to see his aunt, uncle, and four cousins. Dany's mother and father are happy, too. Dany doesn't have any sisters or brothers, and he is sometimes sad because he is alone.

2   "It's not too hot in Casablanca, Dany. It's 22 degrees. Pack the right clothes in your suitcase," says Aunt Regine.

   Dany is glad that Aunt Regine tells him about the weather. Now he can pack the right clothes. What does he pack?

While You Read

A. 1. Look at section 1.

   a. Write the sentence that tells how Dany feels about his visit.
   b. Write the sentence that tells that Dany is an only child.

   2. Look at section 2.

   a. Write the information about the weather in Casablanca.
   b. Write the sentence that tells why Dany is happy to know about the weather in Casablanca.

B. As you read, complete the sentences.

The _____ rings. It's Dany's _____. She invites

_____ to visit for a _____. Dany is _____. He

wants to see his _____, _____, and four

_____. Dany's _____ and _____ are happy,

too. Dany doesn't have any _____ or _____, and he

is sometimes sad because he is _____.

"It's not _____ _____ in Casablanca, Dany. It's 22

degrees. _____ the right _____ in your suitcase,"

says Aunt Regine.

Dany is _____ that Aunt Regine tells him about the

_____. Now he can _____ the right _____.

What does he _____?

C. 1. Write two sentences about section 1 to tell a classmate.
   2. Write two questions about section 2 to ask a classmate.

After You Read

Comprehension Check

A. Work in groups to answer these questions.

1. Does Dany pack the right clothes for his trip? Why or why not?
2. What are two ways of measuring temperature?
3. What countries use the Celsius scale (°C)?
4. What countries use the Fahrenheit scale (°F)?
5. Change 22 degrees Celsius (22°C) to degrees Fahrenheit (°F). Use this formula:
   $9/5 \times °C + 32 = °F$
6. Change 72 degrees Fahrenheit (72°F) to degrees Celsius (°C). Use this formula:
   $(°F - 32) \times 5/9 = °C$
7. What is the temperature in Casablanca in degrees Celsius? in degrees Fahrenheit?
8. What kind of clothes should Dany pack for that temperature?

B. 1. What do you pack in your suitcase for cold weather? for hot weather?

Cold Weather   Hot Weather

2. Is anything the same for both kinds of weather?

C. Imagine that you are Aunt Regine or Uncle Claude. What do you say when you see Dany's clothes? Imagine that you are Dany. What do you say to your aunt or uncle? Work with a classmate to write a dialogue between Dany and his uncle or aunt.

D. Draw your family tree. Explain it to a classmate.

Structure Practice

A. Change these sentences to the negative. Then change them to questions.

Example: It is raining.
 It is not raining.
 Is it raining?

1. The phone rings.
2. Dany is happy.
3. Dany has cousins.
4. It is too hot.
5. Aunt Regine tells Dany about the weather.

B. 1. Using as many adjectives as you can, write a description of Dany.
 2. Exchange and compare descriptions with a classmate. How are they the same? How are they different?

Story 8

On Guard

Before You Read

A. 1. What does the word **museum** make you think of? Write some words.

2. Write three or four sentences using some of your ideas.

B. Look at this list of time periods. They are in chronological order. Choose one time period. Write three sentences about it. Share your sentences with the class.

1. ancient Greece
2. ancient Rome
3. Middle Ages
4. Renaissance
5. Napoleonic Era
6. modern times

C. Match each picture with the correct word or phrase.

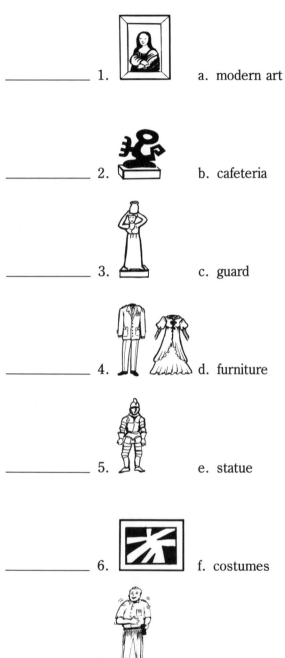

_____ 1.   a. modern art

_____ 2.   b. cafeteria

_____ 3.   c. guard

_____ 4.   d. furniture

_____ 5.   e. statue

_____ 6.   f. costumes

_____ 7.   g. sculpture

_____ 8.    h. armor

_____ 9.   i. painting

D. Answer these questions about the picture on page 50.

1. What do you see in the room?
2. What is the woman doing?
3. Why is the guard laughing?

On Guard

1 Every Sunday the Bakouches visit some interesting place in the city. Today they are at a museum. This museum has statues from ancient Greece and Rome, paintings from the Renaissance, armor worn by knights in the Middle Ages, and costumes from the Napoleanic Era. It also has a gallery of modern art.

2 The museum is very large, so the Bakouches must walk and walk. They all become very tired and decide to go to the cafeteria for a drink.

"Oh, look! There's a guard," says Mrs. Bakouche. "Let's ask him how to get to the cafeteria."

Mrs. Bakouche repeats her question three times, but the guard doesn't answer her. She becomes angry.

"Mom, stop shouting!" says Frank. "That guard can't hear you. We're in the modern sculpture section. You are talking to a statue!"

While You Read

A. 1. Number these historical periods so they are in chronological order.

_____ Middle Ages

_____ ancient Rome

_____ modern times

_____ ancient Greece

_____ Renaissance

_____ Napoleonic Era

2. Now write the names of the periods on this time line.

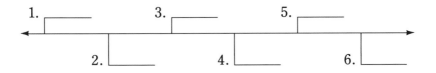

B. 1. Answer these questions about section 1.

    a. What are some things the Bakouche family sees in the museum?

    b. What are some other interesting places the Bakouche family can visit?

2. Answer these questions about section 2.

    a. Why are Mr. and Mrs. Bakouche and Frank tired?

    b. Why does Mrs. Bakouche talk to the guard?

    c. How does Mrs. Bakouche feel at the end of the story?

C. 1. As you read, complete this chart about the story.

persons	
place	
problem	
action	
ending	

2. Using the information from the chart, tell a friend the story. Then write four sentences about the story.

After You Read

Comprehension Check

A. Work with a classmate. Compare your answers for activity D, page 49, with the story.

B. Imagine that the statue guard can talk. Write a dialogue between the statue guard and Mrs. Bakouche. Act out your dialogue with a classmate.

C. Work in groups of five to complete the chart. Share your answers with the class.

1. What kinds of museums are there in your native country?
2. How often did you visit museums in your native country?
3. What did you see?
4. Do you like museums?

	Person				
	1	2	3	4	5
kinds of museums					
frequency of visits					
what you saw					
like/don't like					

Structure Practice

A. Put the time periods in chronological order by writing an ordinal number on each line.

1st   2nd   3rd   4th   5th   6th

_____ modern times

_____ Renaissance

_____ ancient Rome

_____ ancient Greece

_____ Middle Ages

_____ Napoleonic Era

B. Now write sentences that tell which time period comes first, second, third, fourth, fifth, and sixth.

Example: Ancient Greece comes first.

C. Write the plural form of each word.

1. painting
2. furniture
3. knight
4. costume
5. statue
6. armor

It's for the Birds

Before You Read

A. 1. What does the word **hobby** make you think of? Write some words for each category.

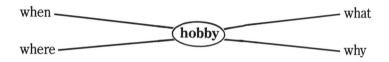

when ——————————— what
(**hobby**)
where ——————————— why

2. Write four sentences using some of your ideas. Compare your sentences with a classmate's.

B. Look at the picture. Write two sentences about the picture that are true and two sentences that are false. Show your sentences to a classmate. Ask your classmate to find the true and false sentences.

C. Circle the words that you know. Work with a partner to find the meanings of the words that you don't know. Use a dictionary if you need help. Write the definition of each word.

paint	hobby	birds	bench
picture	park	next	nest
favorite	ugly	pigeon	lake

54

D. Look at the picture. Work with a classmate to guess what the story is about.

It's for the Birds

Chau: What's your favorite hobby?

Sven: I like to paint, but I don't like this picture.

Chau: Why not?

Sven: It's ugly. The blue looks gray, the red looks brown, and the yellow looks green.

Chau: I think it's pretty.

Sven: No, it's not. It's for the birds.

Chau: What are they going to do with it?

While You Read

A. Circle the word that best completes each sentence about the story.

1. Sven likes to (a) swim (b) paint (c) read.
2. He thinks that his painting is (a) pretty (b) funny (c) ugly.
3. He thinks it's (a) for the girls (b) for the birds (c) for his father.
4. Chau thinks the painting is (a) pretty (b) funny (c) ugly.
5. The picture is ugly because (a) Sven can't paint (b) Sven doesn't like colors (c) the colors aren't good.

B. 1. As you read, complete this chart about the story.

persons	
place	
problem	
action	
ending	

2. Now tell the story to a classmate. Use your chart for help.

C. 1. As you read, complete the sentences.

Sven's favorite hobby is _____. He doesn't like his

_____. The blue looks _____, the _____

looks _____, and the _____ looks _____.

Chau thinks that the picture is _____. Sven thinks that

it's _____.

2. Exchange answers with a classmate and check each other's work.

After You Read

Comprehension Check

A. What is your favorite hobby? Work in groups of five to complete the chart.

Person	Favorite Hobby
1	
2	
3	
4	
5	

B. 1. Compare your answers with the other groups. Complete this chart.

	Group					
	1	2	3	4	5	6
favorite hobbies						

2. What are your classmates' five most popular hobbies? How many people like each one? Show the information in a line graph.

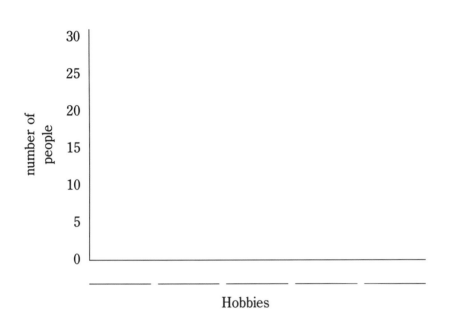

3. Write five sentences about your graph.

   Example: Seven people like skating.

C. Interview a classmate about his or her hobbies. Then report the information to the class. Answer the questions.

D. 1. What is the meaning of **It's for the birds?**
   2. How do you express this idea in your native language?
   3. Why is the picture on page 55 funny?

Structure Practice

A. 1. Write six questions about the picture on page 55, using the words **who, what, when, where, why,** and **how.**

   2. Ask a classmate to answer your questions.

B. Change these sentences to the negative.

   1. I like to paint.
   2. It's ugly.
   3. The blue looks gray.
   4. I think it's pretty.
   5. The birds want the picture.

C. Look at the picture on page 55. Complete the sentences with **There is** or **There are.**

   1. _____ one picture.

   2. _____ two boys.

   3. _____ many pigeons.

   4. _____ one nest.

   5. _____ one lake.

Story 10

Symphony in Zzzzz

Before You Read

A. 1. What does the word **music** make you think of? Write some words.

music

2. Write three or four sentences using some of your ideas.

B. Match each word with its antonym.

1. loudly
2. awake
3. sitting
4. grandfather

a. standing
b. softly
c. grandmother
d. asleep

C. 1. Look at the picture on page 61. Circle the words that describe what you see. Work with a classmate.

asleep	loudly
awake	museum
chorus	orchestra
concert hall	painter
conductor	sitting
grandfather	softly
grandmother	standing

2. Write five sentences about the picture using the words you
   circled.

D. Write three questions about the picture and ask a classmate to
answer them.

Symphony in Zzzzz

Camille's grandfather loves classical music. His favorite music is by the great Russian composer Tchaikovsky. When he goes to a concert, it is always to hear Tchaikovsky's music. He likes the *1812 Overture* the best. Camille often goes with him.

"Grandpa," asks Camille, "why do you always go to Tchaikovsky concerts? Why do you like his music so much?"

"Because much of it is very loud. The louder the music, the louder I can snore."

While You Read

A. 1. Complete the chart.

what Camille's grandfather likes	
where he goes	
what he does	
why he likes loud music	

2. Write four sentences using the information from the chart.

B. Answer the questions.

1. Who was Tchaikovsky?
2. What country was he from?
3. What kind of music did he write?
4. Name a piece of his music.

C. Write the sentences that tell

1. the name of Grandpa's favorite composer.
2. the reason Grandpa likes his music.
3. what Grandpa does when the music is loud.

After You Read

Comprehension Check

A. What else do you want to know about Tchaikovsky? Write three or four questions and share them with the class.

B. 1. Choose a composer you like and complete the chart. Go to the library if you need more information.

name of composer	
date of birth	
country of origin	
living/deceased	
kind of music	
name of a composition	

2. Using the information from your chart, write a short paragraph about the composer. Share it with a classmate.

C. 1. What do you do in a concert hall or theater? Circle yes or no.

a. bring a book to read	yes	no
b. make noise	yes	no
c. listen to the music	yes	no
d. be quiet	yes	no
e. drink soda	yes	no
f. clap your hands at the end	yes	no
g. yell "bravo"	yes	no

2. Compare your answers with a classmate's. Which are the same? Which are different?

Structure Practice

A. Circle your answer for each question.

1. Do you listen to music?
   a. often b. sometimes c. never

2. Do you go to concerts?
   a. often b. sometimes c. never

3. Do you go to sleep while listening to music?
   a. often b. sometimes c. never

4. Do you like to listen to loud music?
   a. often b. sometimes c. never

B. Work in groups of five. Ask each other the questions in activity A.

C. Underline the verbs in the story. Then write a sentence with each verb.

D. Complete this chart of comparative and superlative adjectives.

tall	taller	tallest
	louder	
		best
		most modern
soft		

E. Change these sentences to the negative.

1. Grandpa loves music.
2. He goes to concerts.
3. We like Tchaikovsky.
4. They listen to the symphony.
5. I snore at concerts.

By the Book

Before You Read

A. 1. What does the word **dictionary** make you think of? Write some words.

dictionary

2. Write four sentences using your ideas. Ask a classmate to check your sentences for mistakes in grammar and spelling.

B. Circle the correct word for each picture.

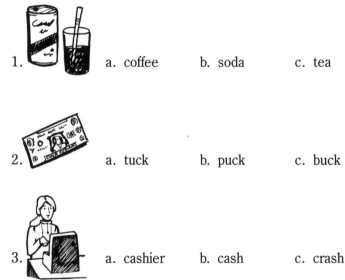

1.   a. coffee   b. soda   c. tea

2.   a. tuck   b. puck   c. buck

3.   a. cashier   b. cash   c. crash

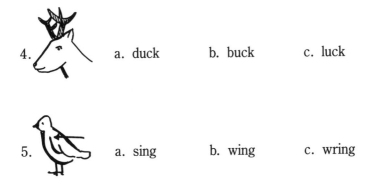

4.   a. duck   b. buck   c. luck

5.   a. sing   b. wing   c. wring

C. Look at the picture on page 68. Write three questions. Exchange papers with a classmate and answer each other's questions.

By the Book

Tat Meng is a new student at Liberty High School. This is his fourth day in the United States. Tat Meng takes his English dictionary everywhere he goes. Today he is buying a soda at the snack bar.

"That's half a buck," says the cashier.

"Half a buck?" Tat Meng is confused. He quickly finds the word *buck* in his dictionary. Then he looks even more confused. "I don't see any deer in here," he says.

Tat Meng's classmate Ashley is in line behind him. "The cashier means you owe fifty cents," Ashley explains. "A *buck* is a slang name for a dollar."

Tat Meng smiles and gives the cashier fifty cents. Then he turns to Ashley. "I guess I can't learn everything about English from a dictionary."

"You're right about that. But don't worry. I'll take you under my wing."

Tat Meng looks confused. He reaches for his dictionary again.

"Oh, put away your dictionary!" Ashley laughs. "I'll teach you all the English you need to know."

While You Read

A. 1. Look for these words in the story. Circle the words you find.

cashier	desk	dictionary
drink	fourth	half a buck
money	pencil	snack bar
soda	student	teacher
test	today	wing

2. Now check your answers with a classmate.

B. Answer these questions while you read.

1. Where is Tat Meng?
2. Where does he go to school?
3. Who helps Tat Meng?
4. What is a buck?
5. What is a cashier?

C. Find a sentence in the story that tells

1. what Tat Meng wants to buy.
2. how much it costs.
3. what Ashley is going to do.

After You Read

Comprehension Check

A. Answer the questions with a classmate.

1. Why does Tat Meng take his English dictionary everywhere he goes?
2. How old is Tat Meng?
3. Why is Tat Meng buying a soda?
4. Why is Tat Meng confused?
5. What is Ashley going to teach Tat Meng?

B. Do people always use money to buy things? What other ways can people pay for things? Talk about your ideas with the class. Then write two or three sentences.

C. 1. What kinds of money do people use in other countries? Ask your classmates and complete the chart.

Country	Money	How much for one dollar

2. Write some sentences with your information.

D. Match the following.

1. 1¢	a. a nickel
2. 5¢	b. a dollar
3. 10¢	c. a dime
4. 25¢	d. a penny
5. $1.00	e. a quarter

E. Write the meaning of each phrase.

1. by the book
2. half a buck
3. to take someone under one's wing

Structure Practice

A. Use these verbs to describe the picture on page 68. Write a sentence with each verb. Then show your sentences to a classmate.

are talking	is buying
is holding	is smiling
is waiting	is asking

B. Circle the best answer for each question.

1. How often do you use your dictionary?
   a. every day   b. never   c. sometimes

2. When do you drink soda?
   a. always   b. sometimes   c. never

3. How often do you see your friends?
   a. sometimes   b. never   c. every day

C. Make these sentences negative. Use the word *never.*

Example: He has enough money.
           He never has enough money.

1. She waits in line.
2. We drink too much soda.
3. I use my dictionary.
4. You look confused.

Letter Litter

Before You Read

A. 1. What does the word **letter** make you think of? Write some words.

letter

2. Compare your ideas with a classmate's. Are they the same or are they different?

Same Ideas   **Different Ideas**

_____   _____

_____   _____

_____   _____

3. Write four or five sentences using some of your ideas.

B. Circle the correct word for each picture.

1.   a. mailbox   b. trash can   c. post office

2.   a. spot   b. slat   c. slot

3.   a. mail chute   b. mailbox   c. trash can

4.   a. litter   b. loiter   c. letter

5.   a. litter   b. letter   c. ladder

6.   a. fire truck   b. sanitation truck   c. police car

7.   a. sanitation worker   b. police officer   c. fire fighter

8.   a. square   b. stump   c. stamp

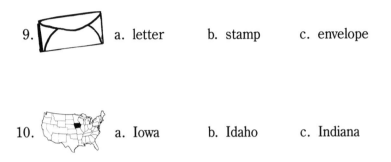

9.   a. letter   b. stamp   c. envelope

10.   a. Iowa   b. Idaho   c. Indiana

C. 1. What is happening in the picture on page 75? Write as many sentences as you can.

    2. Now exchange papers with a classmate. Can you correct or add anything?

D. 1. Answer the questions.

      a. How much does a first-class stamp cost in your native country?

      b. How much does an airmail stamp cost in your native country?

      c. How much do first-class and airmail stamps cost in the United States?

    2. Bring some stamps to show the class.

Letter Litter

1   Yolanda is from Peru. Her family still lives there. A month ago, Yolanda came to live with her aunt, uncle, and three cousins in Rock Creek, Iowa. She is happy in the United States, but she misses her family a lot.

2   One day Yolanda decides to write her family a long letter. It is the first letter that she writes them. When she finishes, she puts her letter in an envelope and puts a stamp on it. Then she quickly goes to mail it.

3   Yolanda asks a man on the street where she can mail her letter. He points toward the corner. Yolanda sees two boxes near the corner. One says **Litter.** The other says **Letters.** They look almost the same. Where do you think Yolanda puts her letter?

While You Read

A. 1. Answer these questions about section 1.

    a. What is Yolanda's native country?
    b. Where does she live now?
    c. Is she happy? Why or why not?

  2. Answer these questions about section 2.

    a. What does Yolanda decide to do?
    b. Is this her first letter to her family?
    c. What does she do when she finishes the letter?

  3. Answer these questions about section 3.

    a. Does Yolanda know where to mail the letter?
    b. Whom does she ask?
    c. Where do you think she puts her letter? Why?
    d. Does her letter arrive in Peru? Why or why not?

B. 1. Read the story again. Underline the words that you do not know. Then work with a partner to find the meanings of the words.
  2. Copy the sentences from the story that contain the new words.

C. 1. As you read, complete the chart.

main character	
where she lives	
what she writes	
where she goes	
whom she asks	
what she does	

2. Using the information from the chart, tell the story to a classmate. Then write the story.

After You Read

Comprehension Check

A. Write a letter to a friend in your native country. Use all or some of these ideas.

(date)→ *(month) (day), (year)*

Dear _____ ,

   How _____ you? I'm _____ . I _____ my family very much. It's very _____ here.

   I live in _____ . This is how it looks. _____

_____

_____

   Every day I _____

_____

On the weekends _____

   School is _____

My teachers _____

The work is _____

After school I _____

   What I like about living here is that _____

_____

What I don't like is that _____

_____

Tell me about yourself. Write soon.

Your friend,

_____

B. Now address the envelope.

┌───┐
│   │
│   │
│   │
│   │
│   │
│   │
│   │
│   │
│   │
└───┘

1. Where do you write your return address?
2. Where do you write your friend's address?
3. Where do you put the stamp?
4. What is a zip code? Where do you write it?
5. Where do you write **airmail** on the envelope?

C. Answer the questions. Go to the post office if you need more information.

1. How much does it cost to mail a letter to someone in the United States?

2. How much does it cost to mail a letter to your native country?
3. How much does it cost to mail a letter to Canada? Puerto Rico? Haiti? Mexico?
4. How much does it cost to mail a letter to Asia? Europe? the Middle East? Africa? South America? Australia?
5. What is an aerogram? How much does an aerogram cost?

Structure Practice

A. Complete the questions with the words **how much** or **how many.**

1. _____ milk do you drink?

2. _____ money does it cost?

3. _____ dollars are on the table?

4. _____ litter is on the floor?

5. _____ letters can I write?

B. Write a command for each sentence.

Example: Tell Susan to throw out the garbage.
Throw out the garbage.

1. Tell Mark to mail his letters now.
2. Tell Tim to write a letter to his cousin.
3. Tell Yolanda to ask the man a question.
4. Tell Beth to put her letters here.

C. Look at the picture on page 75 and complete each sentence with the word **above, below,** or **next to.**

1. The trash can is _____ the mailbox.

2. The word _____ the slot is **Litter.**

3. The sun is shining _____ the buildings.

D. 1. Change one letter of each word to make a new word.

   Example: letter/litter

   truck/_____   same/_____

   slot/_____   live/_____

   miss/_____   but/_____

2. Ask a classmate to write a sentence with each new word.

Get Ready, Get Set, Get Dressed

Before You Read

A. 1. What does the word **clothes** make you think of? Write some
   words.

clothes

   2. Write four sentences using some of your ideas.

B. 1. Look at the picture on page 83. Then read this paragraph.
   Some of the information is not true. Put a line through the
   parts that are not true.

   A man and a woman are sitting on a couch. The woman is

   wearing her bathrobe. She has a bow in her hair. The radio

   is playing. Judy is walking into the living room. She is

   wearing a T-shirt and a skirt. She looks very happy.

   2. Compare your work with a classmate's.
   3. Rewrite the paragraph to make it describe the picture
   correctly.

C. Match each picture with the correct word.

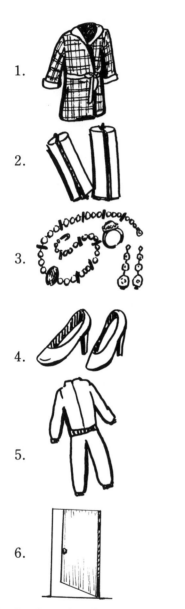

1.   a. jewelry

2.   b. sweatsuit

3.   c. bathrobe

4.   d. doorway

5.   e. curlers

6.   f. high-heeled shoes

D. Look at the picture on page 83 and try to guess what the story is about. Write a short paragraph. Compare your story with a classmate's.

Get Ready, Get Set, Get Dressed

Judy is staying at home tonight. She wants to study, talk on the telephone, and then watch some TV with her mother. Judy comes into the living room and sees her mother sitting in a chair. Her mother is dressed in her bathrobe. She has curlers in her hair. She is also wearing jewelry and high-heeled shoes.

"Why do you have curlers in your hair? Why are you wearing your bathrobe?" asks Judy.

"Why not? Nobody is coming to visit," sighs her mother.

"So why are you wearing your best jewelry and your high-heeled shoes?" continues Judy.

"Maybe somebody is going to come. You never know," answers her mother.

While You Read

A. Answer the questions.

    1. Why is Judy staying at home tonight?
    2. How is her mother dressed?
    3. Where is her mother sitting?
    4. How does Judy feel when she sees her mother?
    5. How do you feel about Judy's mother?

B. Find the antonym for each word or phrase in the story.

    1. going out   6. everybody
    2. standing   7. worst
    3. undressed   8. stops
    4. his   9. always
    5. low-heeled   10. asks

C. 1. Ask a classmate to fill in the missing words as you read the story.

Judy is staying _____ tonight. She wants to

_____, talk on the _____, and then

_____ _____ TV with her mother. Judy

_____ into the living room and _____ her

mother _____ in a _____. Her mother is

dressed in her _____. She has _____ in her

hair. She is _____ wearing _____ and

high-heeled _____.

    2. Check each other's work.

After You Read

Comprehension Check

A. Answer the questions with your own ideas.

    1. Why is Judy's mother dressed like that?
    2. What does Judy want to watch on TV?
    3. Where is Judy's father?
    4. Who is coming to visit Judy's mother?
    5. What does Judy study?

B. Imagine that somebody comes to visit. Write a dialogue between the visitor and Judy's mother. Act out your dialogue with a classmate.

C. Choose a person in the class. Write a description of what she or he is wearing. Don't forget to write the color of the clothing. Read your description to the class and ask the class to guess the person's name. Here are some words to help you.

glasses	pants	jacket	baseball cap
hat	sweater	watch	belt
shirt	sneakers	earrings	blouse
skirt	high-heeled shoes	necklace	gloves
dress	sandals	tie	scarf
shorts	T-shirt	sweatshirt	sweatsuit

Structure Practice

A. 1. Ask a classmate to write all the verbs she or he hears as you read the story about Judy and her mother.

————————   ————————   ————————

————————   ————————   ————————

_____   _____   _____

_____   _____   _____

_____   _____   _____

2. Now ask your classmate to write five sentences using some of the verbs. Check your classmate's work.

B. Circle the correct superlative adjective.

1. Mother is wearing her _____ jewelry.
   a. good   b. better   c. best

2. Seventy is my _____ test mark.
   a. worst   b. bad   c. worse

3. English is the _____ interesting subject.
   a. very   b. most   c. more

4. This problem is _____.
   a. harder   b. hard   c. the hardest

5. Judy is the _____ person I know.
   a. nicer   b. nicest   c. nice

C. Change the verbs in this paragraph to the present progressive tense.

Example: Judy stays at home.
            Judy is staying at home.

Judy stays at home. She listens to music and studies. Her mother sits in the living room. She watches TV. She wears a bathrobe. Judy and her mother wait for people to visit. Nobody comes.

Story 14

A Tacky Situation

Before You Read

A. 1. What does the word **tax** make you think of? Write some
words for each category.

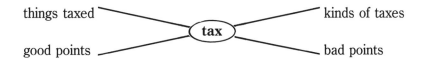

things taxed   kinds of taxes

tax

good points   bad points

2. Write four or five sentences using some of your ideas.

B. 1. Study the picture on page 88. Then close your book. What
do you remember about the picture? Write everything you
can think of.
2. Exchange papers with a classmate and read each other's
work. Did you remember the same things? Look at the
picture again. Which things did you both forget?

C. Work with a classmate to find the meanings of these words.
Use a dictionary if you need help.

1. tax
2. tacks
3. government
4. glue
5. cashier

A Tacky Situation

Chapur is at the drugstore. He is buying a notebook and some glue.

"Three dollars and seventy-six cents, please," says the cashier.

"That isn't right," Chapur says. "Look! The notebook costs two dollars and the glue costs $1.50. The total is $3.50."

"You're forgetting about the tax," the cashier says.

"Tacks? I'm not buying any tacks!"

"No, t-a-x. Sales tax. That's money you pay to the government every time you buy something."

"Oh, I understand," says Chapur. "Okay. The government can have my twenty-six cents. But I think a better idea is to give the government twenty-six tacks."

While You Read

A. As you read, complete the chart.

main character	
where he is	
what he is buying	
what he forgot	
how much he must pay	
how he feels about the government	

B. Write a summary of the story. Use the information on your chart for help.

C. Cross out the information that is not in the story.

Chapur is twenty-two years old. He is at the drugstore. He is next to his school. He is buying a notebook and a bottle of glue.

"Three dollars and seventy-six cents, please," says the cashier. She smiles at Chapur.

"That isn't right," Chapur says. He shows her the prices on the notebook and the glue. "The total is $3.50." Chapur gives her his money.

"You're forgetting about the tax," the cashier says.

Chapur is confused. He isn't buying any tacks. He has some at home.

"No, t-a-x. Sales tax. That's money you pay to the government every time you buy something."

Chapur understands now. He is going to pay the tax. Next time he is going to buy some tacks.

After You Read

Comprehension Check

A. 1. Sit in groups of five and ask each other these questions.

　　a. Are there taxes in your native country?
　　b. What is taxed in your native country?
　　c. Is the tax added to the price of an item or included in
　　　the price?

2. Now complete this chart.

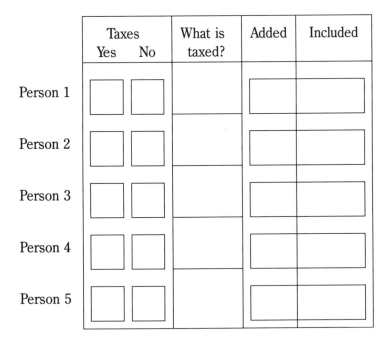

	Taxes Yes No	What is taxed?	Added	Included
Person 1	☐ ☐			
Person 2	☐ ☐			
Person 3	☐ ☐			
Person 4	☐ ☐			
Person 5	☐ ☐			

3. Share your group's answers with the class.

B. How much is the sales tax where you live?

C. Sit with a partner and answer these questions.

1. Thom's dinner costs $26.35. The tax is 8.5% (8½%). How
   much must he pay the cashier?

2. Don buys sneakers for $52.50. He must pay a tax of 6.0%. How much do his sneakers cost with the tax?

3. Maryse's plane ticket to Haiti costs $650. She must pay 5.25% (5¼%) tax. How much does she pay in all?

D. 1. Choose one topic. Write three reasons to support your topic.

Taxes are good.   Taxes are bad.

1.   1.

2.   2.

3.   3.

2. Tell your reasons to a partner. Your partner must tell your reasons to the class.

Structure Practice

A. Find the definitions for each pair of homonyms. Write a sentence for each word. The starred words are in the story.

1. *tacks
   *tax

2. *some
   sum

3. *buy
   by

4. *right
   write

5. *two
   *to

B. Change these sentences to the negative and question forms.

> **Example:** Chapur pays the tax.
> <u>Chapur doesn't pay the tax.</u>
> <u>Does Chapur pay the tax?</u>

1. We must pay taxes.
2. Chapur can understand taxes.
3. The tax rate is 10 percent.

C. Circle the correct answer.

1. It is best to pay your taxes (quick/quickly).
2. The cashier explains about taxes (slowly/slow).
3. She answers the questions (well/good).

D. Write these percentages in numbers.

1. six and a half percent
2. eight and a quarter percent
3. five and a third percent
4. seven and three quarters percent
5. four and a fifth percent

Story 15

Something's Fishy Here

Before You Read

A. 1. What does the word **fish** make you think of? Write some words.

fish

2. Write three sentences using some of your ideas.

B. 1. Name the things that you see in the picture on page 94.

_____ _____

_____ _____

_____ _____

_____ _____

2. Tell a classmate what you see.

C. 1. Draw a picture that shows what happens next.
2. Write two or three sentences about your picture.

Something's Fishy Here

It is Saturday afternoon. There is no school today. Shu Li is fishing. There are many fish in the water. She wants fish for supper. She dreams about a supper of fish, rice, and vegetables.

Suddenly, something pulls on Shu Li's line. Shu Li is very happy. She is sure that it is a fish. She pulls the line out of the water. Surprise! There is no fish on the end of her line. There is an old shoe. Too bad for Shu Li. Now, what is she going to eat for supper?

While You Read

A. 1. Read the story again. Write the words that you do not know.

_____   _____   _____

_____   _____   _____

    2. Work with a classmate to find the meanings of the words. Use a dictionary if you need help.

B. Complete the chart as you read.

person	
time	
place	
action	
ending	
outcome	

C. Write the sentences in the correct order. Add the missing punctuation.

something pulls on her line
it is an old shoe
she is sure that it is a fish
Shu Li is fishing

After You Read

Comprehension Check

A. Write a summary of the story. If you need help, use the
information from your chart in activity B on page 95.

B. Imagine that Shu Li talks with the old shoe. Write a dialogue
between Shu Li and the old shoe. Act out your dialogue with a
classmate.

C. Work in groups of five to answer these questions.

   1. What do you do when there is no school? Do you fish?
   2. In your native country, what did you like to eat for each
      meal? In the United States, what do you like to eat for
      breakfast? lunch? dinner or supper? snacks? Complete the
      charts.

Native Country				
Person	Breakfast	Lunch	Dinner or Supper	Snacks
1				
2				
3				
4				
5				

United States				
Person	Breakfast	Lunch	Dinner or Supper	Snacks
1				
2				
3				
4				
5				

3. Which answers are the same? Which are different? Share your group's answers with the class.

Structure Practice

A. Rewrite the story about Shu Li, changing each affirmative sentence to the negative.

Example: It is Saturday afternoon.
              It is not Saturday afternoon.

B. Circle the correct answers.

1. **There is / there are** a lot of fish.

2. **There is / there are** an old shoe.

3. **There is / there are** no school today.

4. **There is / there are** good things to eat.

5. **There is / there are** a girl fishing.

C. Write five questions using **who, what, when, where,** and **why.** Ask a classmate to answer them.

D. Complete each sentence with **is** or **are**.

1. There _____ school today.

2. There _____ spaghetti for supper.

3. There _____ three fish on the plate.

4. There _____ fish in this lake.

Cold Shoulder

Before You Read

A. 1. What does the word **winter** make you think of? Put these words in the correct categories. Add other words that you think of.

hot chocolate   skiing   ice skates   snow

boots   ice hockey   hot tea   scarf   cold

freezing   sled   **winter**   ice   hat

mittens   soup   gloves   sweater

sleet   snowman   ice skating

blizzard   skis   heavy coat

Weather	Clothing	Food	Sports	Other
snow	sweater	soup	ice hockey	snowman

99

2. Using some of the words on page 99, write a short paragraph about winter.

B. Tell the class about winter in your native country.

1. What is the weather like?
2. What do people wear?
3. What do people do?
4. What did you like about winter in your native country?
5. What didn't you like about it?
6. Compare winter in your native country with winter in the United States.

C. Write everything you can about the picture. Exchange papers with a classmate and check for errors in facts, grammar, and spelling.

D. Look at the picture and try to guess what the story is about. How is it going to end? Write your ideas.

Cold Shoulder

It is winter. Today it is snowing. Everything is soft, quiet, and white. Lanise and William are going to go ice-skating. They decide to go to the lake and not to the rink. The lake is much bigger and prettier. Lanise thinks that it is the prettiest lake in the world.

Lanise thinks that William is the bravest and most interesting boy in the world. She thinks that he can do anything. William is brave and interesting, but he knows that he can't do everything. He doesn't think that skating on the lake is a good idea, but he doesn't want to tell Lanise that he's afraid.

Lanise and William arrive at the lake and put on their ice skates. The ice looks very thick. William isn't afraid anymore. He decides to impress Lanise. He is going to skate near the danger sign. Lanise tells William to stop, but it's too late. Anyway, William can do everything—or can he?

While You Read

A. Find and copy the sentences with these words. With a partner, try to guess the meaning of each word from the sentence.

1. rink
2. brave
3. afraid
4. thick
5. impress

B. Write these sentences in the correct order. Add the missing punctuation.

they go to the lake
william skates on thin ice
lanise and william decide to go skating
they put on their skates
it is winter

C. 1. Find the antonyms of these words in the story.

summer	cowardly
smaller	thin
uglier	take off
loud	early
nothing	leave

2. Write five sentences using some of the antonyms.

D. 1. As you read, complete the chart.

main character	
decision	
where they go	
what they do	

2. Using the information from the chart, tell the story to a classmate.

After You Read

Comprehension Check

A. Sit in groups of five and complete the chart.

	Parents	Teachers	Friends
What do you do to try to impress people?			
When is it good to try to impress people?			
When is it not good to try to impress people?			

B. 1. Write a new ending to the story. Use at least five sentences. Read your ending to the class. Compare it with your answer to activity D on page 100.

   2. Draw a picture of your ending. Compare it with the picture on page 101.

C. Complete this chart about winter sports. Ask a librarian or your classmates, teachers, family members, or friends if you need help.

	Hockey	Ice-skating	Skiing	Other (___)
name of famous athlete				
his/her team or country				
where the sport is played				
special clothing worn				
special equipment used				
if you like to play or watch it				

Structure Practice

A. Change each command to the negative.

> **Example:** Go to the lake!
> Don't go to the lake!

1. Go skating!
2. Skate on thin ice!
3. Try to impress me!
4. Stop!

B. Complete each sentence with the comparative form of the adjective.

Example: Ali is taller than his brother.

1. William is _____ than I am. (brave)

2. Lake Yoohoo is _____ than Lake Gump. (big)

3. Joan and Jane are _____ than Ayelet. (happy)

4. I think history is _____ than math. (interesting)

5. John is _____ than his brother. (afraid)

C. Write six questions about winter, using **who, what, when, where, how,** and **why.** Ask a classmate to answer your questions.

Reading and Riding

Before You Read

A. 1. What does the word **transportation** make you think of?
Write some words.

2. Write five sentences using some of your ideas.

B. Write three true sentences and three false sentences about the
picture. Ask a classmate to find and correct the false
sentences.

C. Look at the picture and guess what the story is about. Write
your ideas and show them to a classmate.

D. In the United States, what kind of transportation do you normally use? In your native country, what kind of transportation did you normally use? Name some old ways to travel. Name some new ways.

Old	New

Reading and Riding

Shafi is new in the United States. On Wednesday, he is going to start school. On Tuesday, his uncle shows him how to take the bus. Shafi learns quickly.

On Wednesday, the first day of school, Shafi's uncle asks him if he remembers how to take the bus.

"Yes. I remember everything," says Shafi.

Shafi's mother gives him money for the bus and says, "Good luck, son. Have a good time in school. Don't forget to ask for a bus pass."

Soon Shafi gets on the bus. He rides and rides. He sees teenagers getting off the bus. They are going to different schools. Shafi can't speak or read English; he can only speak and read Arabic. He doesn't understand the signs; he doesn't remember his phone number; and he doesn't have any more money. He forgets where his school is.

Shafi decides to get off the bus and walk back home. It's cold, but he walks and walks. Finally he sees Avenue I—the only street sign he recognizes. He sees his house and goes in. He is very happy to be home again.

Shafi tells everyone his story. No one believes him. They all laugh.

"You're not in school because you're afraid to go there," they say.

Shafi's uncle decides to take him to school every day for a week. After that, Shafi remembers the way. In the United States, life is much easier if you know English!

While You Read

A. 1. Read the story again. Write the words that you do not know.

———————   ———————   ———————   ———————

———————   ———————   ———————   ———————

———————   ———————   ———————   ———————

2. Copy the sentences containing the new words. Try to guess the meanings of the words. Use your dictionary if you need help.

B. 1. As you read, complete the chart.

where Shafi goes	
how he travels	
what problem he has	
what he does	
what happens in the end	

2. Using the information from the chart, tell the story to a classmate.

C. Number these sentences in the correct order to tell the story.

_____ On Wednesday, Shafi goes alone.

_____ Finally he gets off and walks home.

_____ On Tuesday, his uncle shows Shafi how to take the bus.

_____ Everyone laughs.

_____ He doesn't know where to get off.

_____ Shafi is new in the United States.

After You Read

Comprehension Check

A. Answer the questions.

1. Why does Shafi take the bus alone?
2. Why is Shafi cold?
3. What street does Shafi live on?
4. How do you travel to school?
5. What do you do when you get lost?

B. Write a letter to Shafi. Tell him what to do if he gets lost again, or tell him how to avoid getting lost.

C. Write a dialogue with a classmate. Person A is lost. Person B helps him or her. Act out your dialogue for the class.

D. Compare your answer in activity C on page 106 with the story.

Structure Practice

A. Change these commands to the affirmative.

> **Example:** Don't take a map.
>   Take a map.

1. Don't get off.
2. Don't wear a coat.
3. Don't take the bus.
4. Don't ask questions.
5. Don't go by yourself.

B. Write five commands.

> **Example:** Pick up that paper.

C. Circle the correct form of each verb.

1. He's going _____ school tomorrow.
   a. starts   b. starting   c. to start

2. She's going _____ on the bus.
   a. to get   b. gets   c. getting

3. They're going _____ home.
   a. walking   b. to walk   c. walks

Story 18

Let's Face the Music

Before You Read

A. 1. What does the word **grandparents** make you think of? Write some words.

2. Write four sentences using some of your ideas.

B. Look at the picture on page 114 and circle the best answer for each sentence.

1. This story takes place in _____.
   a. the country b. a big city   c. a village

2. A _____ is playing.
   a. calculator   b. tape recorder c. radio

3. The lady in the picture is _____.
   a. old   b. young   c. middle-aged

4. She is going to throw _____ at the recorder.
   a. an egg   b. a ball   c. a rock

5. She is _____.
   a. happy   b. angry   c. laughing

112

C. Put a check mark next to the words that you know. Work with a classmate to find the meanings of the words that you do not know.

_____ break		_____ pieces	
_____ broken		_____ tape recorder	
_____ continue		_____ turn off	
_____ funny		_____ turn on	
_____ pass		_____ voice	

D. Match the antonyms.

1. turn off	a. sad
2. funny	b. closed
3. first	c. turn on
4. continue	d. last
5. open	e. stop

Let's Face the Music

Dear Kobi,

1   I have a funny story to tell you. It is about my father, Mustafa, and his mother, Nur. In the story, my father is a young man of 21. He decides to go to Riyadh, a big city in Saudi Arabia, to buy a tape recorder.

2   "I am going to be the first person in my village to have a tape recorder," thinks my father. "I want a nice, new tape recorder."

    My father comes home with the recorder, turns it on, and listens to some music. Two hours pass. He goes out to meet some friends, leaving the tape recorder on. He doesn't tell his mother how to turn it off. He doesn't even know that she is home.

My grandmother listens to the music for a while. Then she gets tired. She wants to go to bed.

"Be quiet," she tells the recorder. The music continues. "Be quiet!" she yells. The music continues.

3 Grandmother soon gets very angry because the voices don't listen to her. She goes outside, takes a big rock, and throws it at the recorder. It breaks into a hundred pieces.

"When I say 'be quiet,' why don't you listen?" she shouts.

Soon my father comes back with two friends. He wants to show them the tape recorder. He sees it in pieces on the floor.

4 "What happened?" he asks.

He sees the rock, and he sees an open window. What does he think? Well, Kobi, many years pass before he learns the answer.

Do you have any funny stories to tell me? Write soon.

Love,
Nareen

While You Read

A. 1. As you read, complete the chart.

main characters	
place	
action	
ending	

2. Using the information from the chart, write or tell the story.

B. Find the sentence in the story that

1. tells who this story is about
2. explains why Mustafa goes to Riyadh
3. says what Mustafa does when he comes home
4. tells why Nur gets angry
5. explains what Nur does

C. Write one question for each section of the story. Ask a classmate to answer your questions.

After You Read

Comprehension Check

A. Compare your family with the family in the story. Share your information with a classmate.

	age	dress	attitude toward new things
Nur			
Mustafa			
Your Grandfather or Grandmother			
Your Father or Mother			
You			

B. When he sees the open window and the rock, what does Mustafa think?

C. 1. Many years later, Mustafa's mother tells him about the tape recorder. Write a dialogue between Mustafa and his mother.
   2. With a classmate, act out your dialogue for the class. The class must ask you two questions about it.

Structure Practice

A. Find five infinitives in section 1 of the story. Write a sentence with each one.

Example: to tell   My father likes to tell stories.

B. Find two possessive pronouns in section 2 of the story. Write a question with each one.

Example: my   My grandmother lives in Russia.

C. Find five nouns in section 3 of the story. Ask a classmate to give you an adjective for each one.

Example: music   loud music

D. Find three verbs in section 4 of the story. Write a question with each one to ask the class.

Example: come   Do you come to school by bus?

A Slice of Life

Before You Read

A. 1. What do the words **new in the United States** make you think of? Write some words.

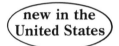

new in the
United States

2. Write a short paragraph using some of your ideas.

B. Make a list of everything you see in the picture. Work with a classmate.

C. Put a check mark next to the words you know. Work with a classmate to find the meanings of the words that you don't know. Use a dictionary if you need help.

_____ as quickly as possible	_____ silent
_____ behind	_____ slice
_____ counter	_____ tray
_____ order	_____ understand
_____ place	_____ young

A Slice of Life

Marie is new in the United States. She sees many places that sell pizza, but she doesn't know how to order it. Her father tells her to ask for a slice of pizza.

All the way to the pizza store, Marie repeats "slice of pizza, slice of pizza, slice of pizza," so that she doesn't forget. In the store Marie asks for a slice of pizza.

The man behind the counter asks, "In or out?"

Marie understands that this is a question, but she doesn't know what it means.

"In," she says.

Soon the man gives her a tray with her pizza. She pays and starts to walk out.

"Hey, young lady," she hears the man call, "where are you going with that tray?"

Marie feels everyone looking at her. She stops, puts down the tray, and runs out of the store as quickly as possible.

When Marie gets home, her father asks, "Where's your pizza?"

Marie is silent. She feels too bad to tell him the story.

While You Read

A. 1. As you read, complete the following.

what Marie wants	
where she goes	
what she asks for	
what the man says	
how Marie feels	
why she leaves	
what she tells her father	

2. Using the information from your chart, tell the story to a classmate.

B. Put a check mark next to the information that you find in the story.

_____ Marie is from Haiti. She's 16 years old.

_____ Marie asks for a slice of pizza.

_____ The man behind the counter is six feet tall.

_____ The man gives Marie sixty cents change.

_____ Marie doesn't want to tell her father the story.

C. Find the antonyms for these words in the story.

old	takes
few	walk in
answer	no one
remember	picks up
in front of	slowly

After You Read

Comprehension Check

A. Work with a classmate. Change the name of the main character
in the story to Jean-Pierre, a boy. What other changes must
you make? Tell your story to the class.

B. Work with a partner. Imagine that one of you is a clerk at a
pizza store and that the other is a customer. What do you say
to each other? Write your dialogue.

C. 1. Work in groups. Talk about the questions and then write
your answers.
a. Why does Marie want pizza?
b. Why doesn't her father go with her?
c. Why is Marie embarrassed?
d. Do you tell your parents everything? Why or why not?

2. Think of an embarrassing experience. Share it with your group.

Structure Practice

A. Combine the sentences using **but.**

Example: Marie likes pizza. It is expensive.
          <u>Marie likes pizza, but it is expensive.</u>

1. She wants to take the bus. She doesn't have any money.
2. Marie pays for the pizza. She leaves it in the store.
3. We want to ask questions. We can't speak English.
4. They are hungry. There isn't anything to eat.

B. As you listen to your teacher read the story, fill in the missing words.

Marie _____ new in the United States. She _____

many places that _____ pizza, but she _____

_____ how _____ _____ it. Her father

_____ her _____ _____ for a slice of pizza.

All the way to the pizza store, Marie _____ "slice of

pizza, slice of pizza, slice of pizza," so that she _____

_____. In the store Marie _____ for a slice of pizza.

The man behind the counter _____, "In or out?"

Marie _____ that this _____ a question, but she

_____ _____ what it means.

"In," she _____.

Soon the man _____ her a tray with her pizza. She

_____ and _____ _____ _____ out.

"Hey, young lady," she hears the man call, "where

_____ you _____ with that tray?"

Marie _____ everyone looking at her. She _____,

_____ down the tray, and _____ out of the store as

quickly as possible.

When Marie _____ home, her father _____,

"Where's your pizza?"

Marie _____ silent. She _____ too bad to

_____ him the story.

C. The missing words in activity B are all verbs. Use as many of
these verbs as you can to write your own story.

Story 20

General Confusion

Before You Read

A. 1. What do the words **history class** make you think of? Write some words.

history
class

2. Write a short paragraph about history class using some of your ideas.

B. Put together these sentences about the American Civil War.

1. The American Civil War began   a. Abraham Lincoln.

2. The Union army of the North fought   b. to leave the Union.

3. The President of the United States was   c. the Confederate army.

4. The Southern states wanted   d. the Union army.

5. George Armstrong Custer was a general in   e. in 1861.

C. 1. Write everything you can about the picture on page 125.

Exchange papers with a classmate. What is the same? What is different? Talk about the picture.

2. Tell your partner what you think the story is going to be about.

General Confusion

There are many stories about George Armstrong Custer. Some of these stories are true, but some are not.

Sometimes people do strange things. This story tells how Custer became a general in the Union army. It takes place around the time of the American Civil War.

"I have to go someplace now. I'm in a hurry. My horse is sick. I'm taking this one," says Custer.

"You can't do that," yells the owner.

"Yes, I can," Custer yells back.

Many hours later, Custer brings back the horse. The horse's owner is still angry. He goes to the army general and tells him about Custer. When the man leaves, the general begins to write a letter to his chief. He is going to tell about Colonel Custer's bad behavior.

In a minute the general has to go and talk to someone. He comes back a little later and finishes the letter: "I recommend Colonel George Armstrong Custer for promotion to general."

What a surprise!

Is this a true story? What do you think?

While You Read

A. Look for these words as you read the story. Work with a classmate to find their meanings. Use a dictionary if you need help.

1. general
2. have to
3. in a hurry
4. owner
5. brings back
6. colonel
7. chief
8. behavior
9. recommend
10. promotion

B. Circle the answer that best completes each sentence.

1. This story takes place in _____.
   a. the United States   b. Puerto Rico   c. Cuba

2. Custer needs a _____.
   a. shave   b. dog   c. horse

3. Custer _____ the animal.
   a. returns   b. keeps   c. feeds

4. The general begins to write a letter
   about Custer's _____.
   a. promotion   b. behavior   c. colonel

5. Someone _____ the general.
   a. interrupts   b. telephones   c. finds

6. The general makes a mistake. He writes
   a letter of _____.
   a. problem   b. permission   c. promotion

C. Find synonyms for these words in the story.

   1. somewhere   6. goes away
   2. in a rush   7. starts
   3. ill   8. actions
   4. shouts   9. ends
   5. returns   10. suggest

After You Read

Comprehension Check

A. Answer the questions. Then share your ideas with a classmate.

   1. Describe Colonel Custer. What kind of man do you think he
      is?
   2. Why does Custer take the horse?
   3. Do you think the general is doing his job well? Why or why
      not?
   4. Do you think Custer is going to be a good general? Why or
      why not?

B. 1. Go to the library. Find the information to complete this chart.

years Custer lived	
what he looked like	
why he is famous	
bad things he did	
good things he did	
your opinion of Custer	

2. Write a paragraph about Custer. Look at your chart for help.
3. Do you think the story about how Custer became a general is true?

C. 1. Think of a famous person from your native country. Complete this chart about him or her.

name	
years she/he lived	
what she/he looked like	
why she/he is famous	
bad things she/he did	
good things she/he did	
your opinion of her/him	

2. Tell the class about your famous person. Use the notes from your chart.

D. Complete this time line about the story.

		The	The	The	The
Custer	Custer	owner	general	general	general
had to...	took...	told...	began...	had to...	forgot...

Structure Practice

A. Change these sentences to the future tense with **going to.** Then change them to the past tense.

Example: This story is about Custer.
   a. This story is going to be about Custer.
   b. This story was about Custer.

1. Custer takes a horse.
2. The owner tells the general.
3. They talk for an hour.
4. The general writes a letter.
5. Custer becomes a general.

B. 1. Write five questions using the future tense with **going to.** Ask a classmate to answer your questions.

Example: Are you going to study tonight?
   Yes, I am.

2. Write five questions using the past tense. Ask a classmate to answer your questions.

Example: Did you eat breakfast today?
   Yes, I did.

C. Match the nouns and pronouns in column A with
   the possessive pronouns in column B.

A	B
1. It's Susan's bag.	a. It's his.
2. The books are Sharon's and Joe's.	b. They're yours.
3. The clothes are yours and Selva's.	c. They're ours.
4. The horse belongs to me.	d. They're theirs.
5. The letter is Craig's.	e. It's mine.
6. The pictures are Ted's and mine.	f. It's hers.

NTC ESL/EFL TEXTS AND MATERIAL
Junior High—Adult Education

Computer Software
Amigo
Basic Vocabulary Builder on Computer

Language and Culture Readers
Beginner's English Reader
Advanced Beginner's English Reader
Cultural Encounters in the U.S.A.
Passport to America Series
  California Discovery
  Adventures in the Southwest
  The Coast-to-Coast Mystery
  The New York Connection
Discover America Series
  California, Chicago, Florida, Hawaii,
  New England, New York, Texas,
  Washington, D.C.
Looking at America Series
  Looking at American Signs, Looking at
  American Food, Looking at American
  Recreation, Looking at American Holidays
Time: We the People
Communicative American English
English á la Cartoon

Text/Audiocassette Learning Packages
Speak Up! Sing Out!
Listen and Say It Right in English!

Transparencies
Everyday Situations in English

Duplicating Masters and
Black-line Masters
The Complete ESL/EFL Cooperative and
  Communicative Activity Book
Easy Vocabulary Games
Vocabulary Games
Advanced Vocabulary Games
Play and Practice!
Basic Vocabulary Builder
Practical Vocabulary Builder
Beginning Activities for English
  Language Learners
Intermediate Activities for English
  Language Learners
Advanced Activities for English
  Language Learners

Language-Skills Texts
Starting English with a Smile
English with a Smile
More English with a Smile
English Survival Series
  Building Vocabulary, Recognizing Details,
  Identifying Main Ideas, Writing Sentences
  and Paragraphs, Using the Context
English Across the Curriculum
Essentials of Reading and Writing English
Everyday English
Everyday Situations for Communicating in
  English
Learning to Listen in English
Listening to Communicate in English
Communication Skillbooks
Living in the U.S.A.
Basic English Vocabulary Builder Activity Book
Basic Everyday Spelling Workbook
Practical Everyday Spelling Workbook

Advanced Readings and Communicative
  Activities for Oral Proficiency
Practical English Writing Skills
Express Yourself in Written English
Campus English
English Communication Skills for Professionals
Speak English!
Read English!
Write English!
Orientation in American English
Building English Sentences
Grammar for Use
Grammar Step-by-Step
Listening by Doing
Reading by Doing
Speaking by Doing
Vocabulary by Doing
Writing by Doing
Look, Think and Write

Life- and Work-Skills Texts
English for Success
Building Real Life English Skills
Everyday Consumer English
Book of Forms
Essential Life Skills series
Finding a Job in the United States
English for Adult Living
Living in English
Prevocational English

TOEFL and University Preparation
NTC's Preparation Course for the TOEFL®
NTC's Practice Tests for the TOEFL®
How to Apply to American Colleges
  and Universities
The International Student's Guide
  to the American University

Dictionaries and References
ABC's of Languages and Linguistics
Everyday American English Dictionary
Building Dictionary Skills in
  English (workbook)
Beginner's Dictionary of American
  English Usage
Beginner's English Dictionary
  Workbook
NTC's American Idioms Dictionary
NTC's Dictionary of American Slang
  and Colloquial Expressions
NTC's Dictionary of Phrasal Verbs
NTC's Dictionary of Grammar Terminology
Essential American Idioms
Contemporary American Slang
Forbidden American English
101 American English Idioms
101 American English Proverbs
Practical Idioms
Essentials of English Grammar
The Complete ESL/EFL Resource Book
Safari Grammar
Safari Punctuation
303 Dumb Spelling Mistakes
TESOL Professional Anthologies
  Grammar and Composition
  Listening, Speaking, and Reading
  Culture

For further information or a current catalog, write:
National Textbook Company
a division of *NTC Publishing Group*
4255 West Touhy Avenue
Lincolnwood, Illinois 60646-1975 U.S.A.